Greetings from
JOLIET
ILL.

Greetings from
JOLIET
ILL.

Greetings from
JOLIET
ILL.

Greetings from
JOLIET
ILL.

Greetings from
JOLIET
ILL.

Greetings from
JOLIET
ILL.

Greetings from
JOLIET
ILL.

Greetings from
JOLIET
ILL.

Greetings from
JOLIET
ILL.

Greetings from
JOLIET
ILL.

Greetings from
JOLIET
ILL.

Greetings from
JOLIET
ILL.

Greetings from
JOLIET
ILL.

Greetings from
JOLIET
ILL.

Greetings from
JOLIET
ILL.

Greetings from
JOLIET
ILL.

Greetings from
JOLIET
ILL.

Greetings from
JOLIET
ILL.

Greetings from
JOLIET
ILL.

Greetings from
JOLIET
ILL.

Greetings from
JOLIET
ILL.

Greetings from
JOLIET
ILL.

Greetings from
JOLIET
ILL.

Greetings from
JOLIET
ILL.

Greetings from
JOLIET
ILL.

Greetings from
JOLIET
ILL.

Greetings from
JOLIET
ILL.

Greetings from
JOLIET
ILL.

Greetings from
JOLIET
ILL.

Greetings from
JOLIET
ILL.

Greetings from
JOLIET
ILL.

Greetings from
JOLIET
ILL.

Greetings from
JOLIET
ILL.

Greetings from
JOLIET
ILL.

Greetings from
JOLIET
ILL.

Greetings from
JOLIET
ILL.

Greetings from
JOLIET
ILL.

Greetings from
JOLIET
ILL.

Greetings from
JOLIET
ILL.

Greetings from
JOLIET
ILL.

Greetings from
JOLIET
ILL.

Greetings from
JOLIET
ILL.

Greetings from
JOLIET
ILL.

Greetings from
JOLIET
ILL.

Greetings from
JOLIET
ILL.

Greetings from
JOLIET
ILL.

Greetings from
JOLIET
ILL.

Greetings from
JOLIET
ILL.

Greetings from
JOLIET
ILL.

Greetings from
JOLIET
ILL.

Greetings from
JOLIET
ILL.

Greetings from
JOLIET
ILL.

Greetings from
JOLIET
ILL.

Greetings from
JOLIET
ILL.

Greetings from
JOLIET
ILL.

Greetings from
JOLIET
ILL.

Greetings from
JOLIET
ILL.

Greetings from
JOLIET
ILL.

Greetings from
JOLIET
ILL.

Greetings from
JOLIET
ILL.

Greetings from
JOLIET
ILL.

Greetings from
JOLIET
ILL.

Greetings from
JOLIET
ILL.

Greetings
from
JOLIET
ILL.

Greetings from
JOLIET
ILL.

Greetings from
JOLIET
ILL.

Greetings from
JOLIET
ILL.

Greetings from
JOLIET
ILL.

Greetings from
JOLIET
ILL.

Greetings from
JOLIET
ILL.

Greetings from
JOLIET
ILL.

Greetings from
JOLIET
ILL.

Greetings from
JOLIET
ILL.

Greetings from
JOLIET
ILL.

Greetings
from
JOLIET
ILL.